LEMUEL HAYNES

THE BLACK PURITAN

LEMUEL HAYNES

THE BLACK PURITAN

LUKE WALKER

He had a deep sense of the awful responsibilities of the ministry, and was "determined not to know any thing among his people save Jesus Christ and him crucified."

Timothy Mather Cooley

WRATH AND GRACE PUBLISHING

Scripture quotations are from The Holy Bible, English Standard Version® (ESV®), copyright © 2001 by Crossway, a publishing ministry of Good News Publishers. Used by permission. All right reserved.

Lemuel Haynes: The Black Puritan, copyright © 2017 by Wrath and Grace Publishing.

ACKNOWLEDGMENTS

Once again, wiser and more learned men than myself have led me by the hand in these studies. Timothy Mather Cooley, Richard Newman, John Saillant, Thabiti Anyabwile, Anthony Carter, Jonathan Den Hartog, and Lemuel Haynes himself are worthy of distinguished note. Thank you.

My publishing and editing team is small but worthy. I express my deepest appreciation for Johan Henao, Franky Collazo, Omri Miles, Brady Erickson, Nick Larson, Zach Larson, Dan Stanley, Sam Stricker, and Carlos Gonzalez. Of course my *more precious than jewels* wife Angel has been my greatest encourager and helpmeet. Many thanks to my local church family, and especially to my co-elder Gottfried Caspari.

Glory be to God for his wisdom and grace in raising up such men as Lemuel Haynes. May he form Christ in us as he has done in the saints who have gone before us.

Dedicated to
my brothers
Alexander Wade
Omri Miles

INTRODUCTION

History is full of forgotten gems. Modern meme scholars know nothing of the intricate, nuanced, and very real treasures it has to offer. Lemuel Haynes is one such hidden jewel. He defies categorization. "Paradox is a concept that goes some distance as a means to understanding much of Haynes' long and unusual life."[1] The Black Puritan is a *problem* for our oversimplified thinking; he refuses to play nice with our broad-brush sense of American history. I have found him to be a breath of fresh air. I believe that, in Mr. Haynes, my readers will meet an unexpectedly refreshing troubler in Israel. I would go so far as to say that he is perhaps *the* elephant in the American room.

In writing, my pen has been animated by the desire of Haynes' first biographer, Timothy Mather Cooley: "At least, it is believed that the friends and admirers of Mr. Haynes, who often listened to the impassioned eloquence of the living preacher, will welcome this attempt to rescue his name from oblivion."[2] This is not a man to be forgotten; and yet, I wonder who of my readers has heard of him? Is not the story that follows worthy of wide publication? If

---

[1] Richard Newman, *Black Preacher to White America* (Brooklyn: Carlson Publishing Inc., 1990), xi.
[2] Timothy Mather Cooley, *Sketches of the Life and Character of the Rev. Lemuel Haynes* (New York: John S. Taylor, 1839), viii.

but one young soul is moved to serve Christ by this little volume, my labors will be infinitely rewarded beyond merit and measure.

Luke Walker
Richfield, MN
June 2017

LEMUEL HAYNES
THE BLACK PURITAN

It's 1753 and our friend Olaudah Equiano is still a happy child in Africa. We are in West Hartford, Connecticut, where a white Scottish indentured servant is fleeing, as though in secret. She's pregnant. Entering a house, she gives birth to a baby boy who is the unwanted offspring of a forbidden crossing of racial lines. She abandons him to the head of the house, a man named Haynes, and vanishes. Haynes names the boy *Lemuel*, which is of course a biblical name. Lemuel was a king who relayed instructions that his mother had given him.[1] Haynes' given name was clearly a jab at his mother for not giving her son any instruction, or anything at all for that matter. And yet, what a wise ruler this child was to become. Well known in life, he remains, like his namesake, an unknown king to this day.

Jonathan Edwards is finishing his course, the free sons of Columbia are waxing warm against the Crown, and slavery and racism cast their shadow over much of American life. Lemuel Haynes was a man born strategically in time, wedged as it were between these influences, pressed by them into a diamond-tipped iron stylus, and destined to inscribe

---

[1] Proverbs 31:1.

HOLY TO THE LORD on the souls of men. He was the American Black Puritan.

EARLY LIFE

Lemuel Haynes took his status in society from his mother, and thus, he became an indentured servant. He was taken in by David Rose, a deacon, and grew up working for the family. Embraced as a member, it was said that Mrs. Rose loved Lemuel more than all her own children.[1]

Young Lemuel had a poor education. Thus—and this will be the mark upon his life—he was self-taught from his earliest days. He rose from deep obscurity to great prominence in his generation. His biographer, pondering such rises to preeminence, says, "It will usually be found, in such cases, that the degree of eminence attained, other things being equal, is in proportion to the amount of difficulty overcome."[2] This correspondence will be found in Haynes' life, whose difficulties were many.

As lore has it, "Lemuel Haynes got his education in the chimney corner."[3] When all his day's work had ceased, he repaired himself to the fireplace, seeking to steal, with the last moments of the day, a morsel

---

[1] Timothy Mather Cooley, *Sketches of the Life and Character of the Rev. Lemuel Haynes* (New York: John S. Taylor, 1839), 30.
[2] Ibid., xvii.
[3] Ibid., 36.

of knowledge. "I make it my rule," he said as a boy, "to know something more every night than I knew in the morning."[1] While his friends played, young Lemuel was preparing for his life's work. Many have expressed on their deathbed the wish to have prayed more in life; Lemuel Haynes was of the sort who wished he had studied more. This was the genius of Lemuel Haynes: he was eminently a *free thinker*. Great works were being prepared for him. Predestined to see more deeply into the principles that were handed down to him than even his forebears, he became, as the psalmist has it, *wiser than his teachers*.

The greatest of all earthly privileges fell to Haynes: he grew up in a godly home. After passing through deep conviction of sin as a young man, he believed on the Lord Jesus Christ. "One evening, being under an apple-tree mourning my wretched situation, I hope I found the Saviour. I always visit the place when I come to Granville, and when I can, I pluck some fruit from the tree and carry it home: it is sweet to my taste. I have fears at times that I am deceived, but still, I *hope*."[2]

---

[1] Ibid., 37.
[2] Ibid., 41.

THE BLACK REPUBLICAN

You may now sling your rifle over your shoulder. In the flower of youth, Haynes served as a minuteman in the Revolutionary War under the leadership of General George Washington, acquiring much of his enduring political ideology. "He," speaking of himself, "devoted all for the sake of freedom and independence…and has never viewed the sacrifice too great. Should an attack be made, as formerly, on this sacred ark, the poor remains of his life would be devoted to its defence; and he is sure he speaks the language of his brethren in the ministry."[1] He believed that "Americans resisted enslavement just as Englishmen had resisted Roman Catholic moves against Protestant liberties."[2] (*Salute*, Master Wycliffe, and Protector Cromwell, as we may perhaps come to find out.)

Waxing warm against unjust wars and aggressions in later life, he used a striking example that shows us how the warrior in him lived on. He asks, if a British soldier committed an unlawful search and seizure upon him, "Will love without dissimulation dispose me to blow out his brains, or

---

[1] Richard Newman, *Black Preacher to White America* (Brooklyn: Carlson Publishing Inc., 1990), 169.
[2] John Saillant, *Black Puritan, Black Republican* (New York: Oxford University Press, 2003), 52.

fracture his skull with the end of my whip, loaded with death?"[1] The answer was of course *No,* but it may be that the example furnishes proof why many believed that the legacy of the Revolution which he continued to embody was "too riotous."[2] Haynes was wont, it would seem, to *bring the ruckus*[3] even unto old age.

As a young man, he wrote an essay titled *Liberty Further Extended,* in which he took the principles of the American Revolution and applied them to slavery. Of course, this was the great irony of the American Revolution. "How is it," asked their British opponents, "we hear the loudest yelps for liberty among the drivers of Negroes?"[4] Could they not see the elephant in the room? Perhaps not, but in Haynes they met a giant who never forgot, whose tusks were of ebony, and whose heavy tread shook the false ground upon which they stood. "Haynes' mature republicanism…dealt with the problem of a slave society committed to freedom, in which slaves were even more abject than in other slaveholding states."[5]

---

[1] Newman, *Black Preacher,* 156-57.
[2] Ibid., 170.
[3] *The RUKUS,* rather.
[4] Samuel Johnson, quoted in Vincent Caretta, *Equiano, the African: Biography of a Self-Made Man* (New York: Penguin Books, 2005), 214.
[5] Saillant, *Black Puritan,* 60.

Liberty Further Extended opened up this irony by contending for just this very thing—extending the liberty of the Revolution to include slaves. Tyranny yet resided *within* America (as Luther's inward pope, or the Belbury old Dimble carried within himself), and this was the most important battle of all. "It cannot Be tho't impertinent for us to…See, whether…we Do not find the monster Lurking in our own Bosom."[1] What did it matter if America had overthrown her outward oppressors? It was but to whitewash tombs; all manner of oppression festered within. "We shall find that subsisting in the midst of us, that may with propriety be stiled *Opression,* nay, much greater opression, than that which Englishmen seem so much to spurn at. I mean an oppression which they themselves impose upon others."[2] To the young black revolutionary, "the abolition of the slave trade and of slavery and the acceptance of black Americans as citizens was inherent in the Revolution."[3]

Lemuel Haynes was a *Federalist,* George Washington being his political hero. In fact, Washington was held in the highest regard by early black abolitionists because in his death he had freed his slaves and renounced slavery. In a speech

---

[1] Newman, *Black Preacher*, 17.
[2] Ibid., 18-19.
[3] Saillant, *Black Puritan,* 116.

honoring Washington's birthday, Haynes says, "He was an enemy to slaveholding, and gave his dying testimony against it, by emancipating, and providing for those under his care. O that his jealous surviving neighbors would prove themselves to be his legitimate children, and go and do likewise!"[1] He goes on: "May we not hail this happy day, that gave birth to our beloved Washington! And raise a tribute of thanks to heaven for so great a blessing!"[2]

As opposed to the Federalists stood Thomas Jefferson. Men like Jefferson had "carried their political philosophy to antiblack extremes" and pushed for colonization, "a manifestly antirepublican solution to slavery and inequality."[3] Haynes fiercely opposed these policies. We find a sampling of his undying opposition in another tribute he raised. In old age, he wandered by mistake into a party in honor of Democrat Andrew Jackson's appointment to the presidency. Before he could *get out* he was urged to make a toast, to which he obliged. He lifted a cup and said, "Andrew Jackson, Psalm 109 verse 8," and they drank heartily.[4] It wasn't until later that somebody bothered to look up the reference, which says, "Let his days be few, and let another take his office."

---

[1] Newman, *Black Preacher*, 167.
[2] Ibid., 168.
[3] Saillant, *Black Puritan*, 49.
[4] Newman, *Black Preacher*, xv.

What was the Jeffersonian political position? It was freedom unbounded, what might be called *the generic liberty of the conscience*. "Jeffersonianism represented to Haynes freedom without restraint."[1] Small central government, maximum freedom to the states and to the people—it all sounds very nice maybe, but Haynes and others foresaw problems, as we ourselves will see presently.

Federalists saw Jeffersonian democracy as nothing short of an infiltration of the Bavarian Illuminati into the United States, the force they believed to be behind the atheistic French Revolution and lurking within freemasonry. One Federalist "suggested that much of Jefferson's theorizing came from his time in France… 'where…his skepticism in religion, morals, and government acquired full strength and vigor.'"[2] This godless anarchy threatened "to destroy American liberties"[3] and the kind of righteous society which a republic required. It tended ultimately to "anarchy, and military despotism."[4]

Unbounded *democracy* was a problem because, in a society of sinners, the masses will inevitably

---

[1] Saillant, *Black Puritan*, 127.
[2] William De Saussure, quoted in Jonathan J. Den Hartog, *Patriotism & Piety: Federalist Politics and Religious Struggle in the New American Nation* (Charlottesville: University of Virginia Press, 2015), 151.
[3] Ibid., 54.
[4] Ibid., 56.

trample upon the rights of the minority. To what shall we liken pure democracy? It is like three wolves and two lambs voting on what to eat for lunch. Combine this kind of majority rule with the fact that democratic leaders like Thomas Jefferson "gazed with horror at a future black American population,"[1] and we may easily see how dangerous *three fifths* can be. It is a strange liberty indeed which ensures the existence of slavery.

This is precisely why early abolitionists like Haynes and Equiano saw the need for a decisive flex of central government power to overthrow slavery. "As the leaders of the black Atlantic forged their abolitionism, they came to understand that only national political institutions had the power to move effectively against the slave trade and slavery."[2] For instance, "Absolom Jones…saw the abolition of the Atlantic slave trade as a further exercise of benevolent statesmanship."[3] They knew that apart from such a move, abolition would be prevented from running its happy course. Of course, they were right; the Civil War has taught us as much. "Several generations before the Civil War, black abolitionists perceived that local or voluntary efforts were never to eradicate the system of slavery."[4]

---

[1] Saillant, *Black Puritan*, 20.
[2] Ibid., 145.
[3] Ibid., 147.
[4] Ibid., 145.

It is somewhat in vogue to believe that slavery was not in fact central to the Civil War; a merely cursory reading of the secession documents of the Southern states is enough to explode this modern myth. They state very plainly that what was at stake for them was their most holy institution, I almost said *religion,* of black slavery.[1] In fact, if we mourn (as we ought to) the hundreds of thousands of able-bodied men lost in America's civil war, but care not a straw for the millions of men, women, and children marred and murdered by race-based slavery, we have yet to face the same elephant in the modern room.

As a Federalist, Haynes believed that the role of government was to maintain social order not simply by protecting a generic freedom of conscience for the masses, but to ensure *the natural rights* of every citizen. The civil authority was to be a republic which protected the individual from the mob. An offer they couldn't refuse was needed; strong central government was required to give it. What was it that Haynes saw as the God-given natural rights of every human being? *Life, liberty, and the pursuit of happiness.* [2]

---

[1] As a sampling, Mississippi says: "Our position is thoroughly identified with the institution of slavery." Virginia, with almost delicious irony (were the matter not so grave), speaks of "the oppression of the Southern Slaveholding States." "The Declaration of Causes of Seceding States," https://www.civilwar.org/learn/primary-sources/declaration-causes-seceding-states.

[2] Ironically (this is quickly becoming an advanced study in irony), words penned by Thomas Jefferson. In the end, it would seem that Thomas was not a Thomist.

As James Madison has it in *The Federalist Papers*, "If men were angels, no government would be necessary."[1] As intriguing as it may be to engage with absolute libertarian anarchocapitalism, the fact of the matter is, such a system will never work in a world inhabited by depraved men. There must be restraints of one kind or another.

These restraints were to be extended to the government itself. Haynes was no statist. In *Dissimulation Illustrated*, he spoke against "unlimited submission to civil authority"[2] and called for defiance to the magistrate where basic rights were violated. "To suppose that their power is *unbounded*, and must not be opposed, let their measures and edicts be ever so unreasonable, is reviving the old tory spirit that was among us in our old revolutionary war."[3] I remind you that these are *Protestant* studies, and the following quote may keep us on track: "No weapon has been more used and more successful in the days of persecution, than the doctrine of passive obedience and non-resistance. Popes, priests, and cardinals were devoted to this business, and were greatly caressed and rewarded by those in authority."[4]

---

[1] The Federalist 51, http://www.let.rug.nl/usa/documents/1786-1800/the-federalist-papers/the-federalist-51.php.
[2] Newman, *Black Preacher*, 152.
[3] Ibid., 155.
[4] Ibid., 154-55.

James Madison says again, "I understand a number of citizens…are united and actuated by some common impulse of passion, or of interest, adversed to the rights of other citizens."[1] A faction or movement within society would then be capable of trampling the freedom of others. The Federalists believed the role of government was to protect the natural rights of every citizen by restricting such factions. James Madison for his part primarily sees the protection of religious, political, and economic rights in this; Haynes sees slavery and racism as just those very problematic interests that are hostile to fellow citizens. Generic freedom of conscience was not enough. "Men can make conscience," he says, "of almost any thing to carry a point. The scriptures speak of a *seared* and *defiled* conscience."[2] Surely, to protect the unbounded freedom of *that* conscience is inevitably to bind the God-given freedom of others.

Early America was already just this sort of factious society. For instance, a gentleman visiting Boston noted "that in all the places he had been in, he never saw so cruel behaviour in all his life, and that a slave in the West-Indies, on Sundays or holidays enjoys himself and friends without molestation."[3] Well, apparently Olaudah Equiano

---

[1] The Federalist 10, http://www.let.rug.nl/usa/documents/1786-1800/the-federalist-papers/the-federalist-10.php.
[2] Newman, *Black Preacher*, 79.
[3] Saillant, *Black Puritan*, 122.

had never been to *Boston,* in the land of the free.[1] A society with such tendencies in its infancy was bound to tear itself apart. Eyeing the trouble, Haynes spread his wings, surveyed Federalism and went *further up and further in,* searching out its inherent abolitionist and pro-black potential.

Up to this point in our studies we've primarily looked at the issue of slavery, but another question looms large, and that is, *what happens in a post-slavery society?* "The first black abolitionists were as much postslavery as they were antislavery thinkers, and they always worried about protection in the future for the newly freed. Their loyalist and Federalist politics flowed from such worries."[2] Here we expand our horizons and follow Lemuel Haynes deep into the essence and implications of republicanism and, as we will see, of Calvinism as well. According to Haynes, a true republic required an egalitarian society fueled by benevolence among its citizens. "The essential feature of Haynes' black republicanism was his insistence that both liberty and benevolence must cross race lines if the republic were to thrive."[3]—that is, *liberty* in the abolition of slavery and *benevolence* among ethnicities.

---

[1] "Every part of the world I had hitherto been in seemed to me a paradise in comparison of the West Indies." *The Interesting Narrative of the Life of Olaudah Equiano* (Peterborough: Broadview Literary Texts, 2004), 135.
[2] Saillant, *Black Puritan,* 179.
[3] Ibid., 163.

He saw republican government as consisting of public servants, elected for the good of society. On the 25th anniversary of Independence Day[1] he delivered an address titled *The Nature and Importance of True Republicanism*. It was essentially a sermon on Luke 22:26. He saw in this text that true greatness is to serve others; in this case, in representative, republican government. In fact, he saw republicanism as a Christian form of government wherein public servants are empowered to seek the good of the people, and to "destroy those distinctions among men that ought never to exist."[2] Elected officials listen to the people and yet, are equipped and given authority to lead the people. The concept is not unlike an elder led church, or better yet, Haynes' own congregationalism.[3]

In the Forgotten War of 1812, white Americans had been taken into slavery by British forces. And, of course, this caused a blood-curdling cry to go forth from the States. In a sermon titled *Dissimulation Illustrated*[4] Lemuel Haynes pointed once again to the elephant in the room—with its great tusks of *irony* – and asked, Excuse me sirs, what about *these* American

---

[1] "By the 1790s the Fourth of July had become an abolitionist holiday celebrated by black New Englanders." Ibid., 60.
[2] Newman, *Black Preacher*, 80.
[3] A system of church government which vested authority ultimately in the people. The New Divinity men were Congregational.
[4] Dissimulation is the old Authorized for *hypocrisy*.

slaves? He quoted a fellow minister in the matter: "Our president can talk feelingly on the subject of impressment of our seamen. I am glad to have him feel for them. Yet in his own state, Virginia, there were, in the year 1800, no less than three hundred forty-three thousand, seven hundred ninety-six human beings holden in bondage for life!"[1] It was, as we might say, *Hypocrisy Further Extended*. "Partial affection, or distress for some of our fellow-creatures, while others, even under our notice, are wholly disregarded, betrays dissimulation."[2] *Some* slavery mattered in America, but not slavery itself. Such bias was squarely opposed to the principled republic America claimed to be.

In his fight for justice, Lemuel Haynes fortified himself with arguments from republicanism. The Black Republican exploited and mined the riches of Federalist republicanism for all its pro-black elements. "The black cause was like the 'Conceal'd Gospel' in the Jewish texts—inherent in republicanism but unrealized in a slaveholding society."[3] In fact, many Federalists, especially those who held their Christianity and politics closely together, mightily denounced slavery.

---

[1] Worcester, quoted in Newman, *Black Preacher*, 157.
[2] Ibid., 157.
[3] Saillant, *Black Puritan*, 53.

Yet, for all its promise, Federalism was oustripped by the new democratic philosophy. The tide was turned, and its proponents turned their efforts to volunteerism. Rooted out of the political sphere, Federalists like Elias Boudinot "hoped to preserve the nation by the most permanent means he could think of—conversion."[1] And thus republicanism, formidable as it is, was far from Haynes' only weapon. A mightier sword he did swing in battle.

THE BLACK PURITAN

Lemuel Haynes was a Calvinist of the *New Divinity* stripe, i.e. *Edwardsean*. He lived during the theological era of Jonathan Edwards. "To see what Jonathan Edwards' theological brilliance would look like in an African American context, we need only to read and understand Lemuel Haynes."[2] He was the black Jonathan Edwards; or, taking into account his greater theological consistency, it seems better to call him *Jonathan Edwards 2.0*. He was perhaps the most thoroughly American Puritan.

While it is not technically accurate to refer to the New Divinity men as Puritans—the Englishmen of

---

[1] Den Hartog, *Patriotism & Piety*, 115.
[2] Anthony J. Carter, *On Being Black and Reformed: A New Perspective on the African-American Christian Experience* (Phillipsburg: P&R Publishing, 2003), 78.

the high orthodoxy era lay strict claim to that title—I have not shied away from the term. *The Black New Divinity Theologian* just doesn't have the same ring to it. What a wiser than I said of Edwards, I will unashamedly say of Haynes: he "was a Puritan in theology and piety."[1]

He was first of all a godly man. It was said that his godliness shone more in his home than out of it—sadly that is most often where our ungodliness is unmasked. With his beloved wife, and among his many children, this king among preachers walked with integrity in his household.[2] He was also a man of the Book. "He studied the Bible till he could produce by memory most of the texts which have a bearing upon the essential doctrines of grace; and could also refer, with nearly infallible accuracy, to the book, chapter, and verse where they might be found."[3] He was a sanctified swordsman.

As a New England Puritan he was, above all things else, *a preacher*. His calling revealed itself in the following manner. The Rose household was in the habit of gathering to hear a sermon read on Saturday evenings, in preparation for Lord's Day worship. Lemuel was the reader, and was in the custom of delivering sermons by Edwards, Whitefield, etc. One

---

[1] Joel R. Beeke and Mark Jones, *A Puritan Theology: Doctrine for Life* (Grand Rapids: Reformation Heritage Books, 2012) 4.
[2] Psalm 101.
[3] Cooley, *Sketches*, 37.

night it seemed to Deacon Rose that there was extraordinary energy in Lemuel's delivery, and he inquired as to the penman. Was it Edwards? *No, it wasn't Edwards.* Whitefield, then, surely. *Not Whitefield either.* Rose kept pressing the young man, to which he finally replied, It was *Lemuel.* He had written a sermon on John 3:3, *You Must Be Born Again,* which can be read to this day. It has become known as *the Saturday evening sermon.* Unable to distinguish it from a Whitefield or an Edwards, the family and the community sprung into full support of the young exegete. "It was now discovered by a discerning Christian community, that in this young man were the germes of usefulness."[1]

He never received formal training. "I was solicited by some to obtain a collegiate education," but the young preacher declined and was instead trained under local church pastors. He imitated these men of God in speech, conduct, love, faith, and purity. Daniel Farrand was his chief instructor, and left indelible marks up the young minister. "In him were blended the deepest piety and the most amusing wit…Such was the structure of Mr. Haynes's mind, that he readily caught the spirit and habits of his early instructor."[2] He forever bore the impress of this teacher. "The unfeigned and vivid piety, together

---

[1] Ibid., 59.
[2] Ibid., 60-61.

with the propensity for satirical and humorous remark, so conspicuous in the instructor, seem to have been transfused into the very soul of the pupil."[1]

He studied Latin under Farrand, and later Greek under William Bradford. His eager spirit drank up the apostolic language. "As a critic on the Septuagint and Greek Testament, he possessed great skill."[2] His training complete, he was subsequently examined and recommended by a body of ministers, and called to the pulpit in Granville, New York. He was the first African American pastor to be ordained by an official denomination, and was probably the first black pastor of an all-white church.

Lemuel Haynes spent decades in the pulpit. He labored long and bore much enduring fruit. He was immensely useful in the cause of God, and, wherever he preached, the room was packed. "He was singularly successful in filling the house of God with attentive and deeply-interested hearers."[3] Oh that God would send us more Lemuels, men who can *hold the hell-bound spellbound!*[4]

He became famous for his piercing wit and iron logic. "He had a disposition for amusing remark and

---

[1] Ibid., 62.
[2] Ibid., 63.
[3] Ibid., 80.
[4] A phrase coined by Leonard Ravenhill.

keen retort."[1] The New England of his time was a place of great skepticism and unbelief, and this stripe of atheists were called *infidels*. He was fitted for the task with his iron logic and quick wits. Once he was called to preach a meeting in another town and nobody showed up. They all said they were too busy. He puzzled, since they couldn't find time to go to a meeting, how they would find time to *die*. Cooley relays another example for us:

> It is said that some time after the publication of his sermon on the text, "Thou shalt not surely die," two reckless young men having agreed together to try his wit, one of them said—"Father Haynes, have you heard the good news?"—"No," said Mr. Haynes, "what is it?"—"It is great news, indeed," said the other, "and, if true, *your* business is done."—"What is it?" again inquired Mr. Haynes. "Why," said the first, "the devil is dead." In a moment the old gentleman replied, lifting up both his hands and placing them on the heads of the young men, and in a tone of solemn concern, "Oh, poor fatherless children! what will become of you?"[2]

---

[1] Cooley, *Sketches*, 61.
[2] Ibid., 123.

To give my readers some flavor of his pen game—and to place it beyond the pale of doubt that in Lemuel Haynes we meet with the spirit of the old Puritans—in *Liberty Further Extended* he took proslavery arguments and said, "which arguments, I shall Endeavor to Shew, are Lame."[1] His chief concern was piety. One of his favorite words in his letters was *stupid;* he used it to indicate spiritual dullness. "We are," he was wont to say, "a stupid people."

Well, by a turn of phrase we might say that his preaching was most *stupid*. "His sermons you could never forget," says one of his hearers.[2] "The essential, humbling doctrines of grace were the seasoning of all his sermons," says Cooley.[3] "His text rarely comprised more than one verse, and in many instances only a single clause."[4] *I like him.* "Although he followed the method of the old divines in the multiplicity of his divisions, yet he never said 8thly or 9thly without a thought that richly rewarded the attention of the hearer."[5] Another says, "You would be carried along through the several divisions of the discourse as by the charm of a musical instrument."[6]

---

[1] Newman, *Black Preacher*, 24.
[2] Cooley, *Sketches*, 292.
[3] Ibid., 79.
[4] Ibid., 293.
[5] Ibid., 293.
[6] Ibid., 292.

The word of God was designed to be preached by living voices in waking life; Haynes' own preaching fulfilled the divine intent and was best experienced firsthand.

Of his physical appearance at the sacred desk we have some knowledge. His only hand motion—and in this department he was regrettably weak—was that his left hand, in which he held his Bible, would move horizontally back and forth (alas! we all have weaknesses). As to his facial expression, he wouldn't look anyone in the eye—of which there was often not a dry specimen in the room[1]—but stood gazing off, as though peering into another world.

He was an extemporaneous preacher. We do have some of his sermons recorded, but most of them were written by his hand as manuscripts. We do not, however, have much vestige of what his live preaching in the pulpit would have been like. There is one sermon, however, that has come down to posterity. It was preached against universalism,[2] and the event fell out as follows:

A universalist preacher named Hosea Ballou, by some strange providence, was scheduled to preach at Haynes' church while he himself was away preaching elsewhere. He boasted that, wherever he preached,

---

[1] "Dr. Dwight, sitting in the pulpit with the speaker, was observed to be deeply affected, even to tears." E.K. Hazen, quoted in ibid., 162.
[2] The belief that all will be saved.

"the orthodox gentry generally *scud*."[1] When Haynes and those with him heard of it, they shut down their own meeting and repaired thither to hear the great universalist. When Ballou saw him, he invited Haynes to ascend the pulpit after himself and say a word or two, which he at first declined. But, incessantly pressed, "Mr. Haynes remarked that he might perhaps be willing to make some remarks."[2]

When Ballou was through, Haynes stood up in the pulpit and *off the top* delivered a seething sermon from Genesis 3, *you shall not surely die*. It was a purely extemporaneous sermon, and perhaps his finest (certainly his most well-known). His biographer says, "No one pretends to give any account of the number of editions that were printed." Modern historians put it at about *seventy*. Those who heard it wrote down what they could, while others say the best of his remarks were lost.

In it, he obliterated the universalist doctrine; the *love wins* preacher, shall we say, got his bell rung. He pictured the devil for the old preacher that he is, and how he came to Eve and preached the very universalist doctrine that Ballou had just finished expounding. "He is a very laborious, unwearied preacher. He has been in the ministry almost six thousand years, and yet his zeal is not in the least

---
[1] Cooley, *Sketches*, 97.
[2] Ibid.

abated."[1] Ballou seemed to think well enough of himself as a popular preacher, but Haynes reminded him of a greater heretic than even he, and that "no preacher can command hearers like him."[2]

The devil's empty promise of life he calls, "Bold assertion! without a single argument to support it."[3] He unmasked the old heresy: "What Satan meant to preach was, that there is no hell; and that the wages of sin is not death, but eternal life."[4] Inferences he drew many, one of them being this: "Was there no truth in future punishment, or was it only a temporary evil, Satan would not be so busy in trying to convince men that there is none."[5]

Ballou wrote to Haynes in the aftermath, and they crossed swords of pen and ink. The champions strove thus one with another, but not without Haynes getting some capital shots in. "You call my discourse 'fraught with *low cunning*.' Sir, when you will show the difference between *low* cunning and *high* cunning, perhaps I shall be able to determine to which of these cunnings your answer to such a piece belongs."[6] Ballou seemed doubly astonished that the matter had first occurred and then gone to print.

---

[1] Ibid., 100.
[2] Ibid., 101.
[3] Ibid.
[4] Ibid.
[5] Ibid., 103.
[6] Ibid., 107.

"Sir," returned Haynes, "the piece has gone through several editions—some of them through my approbation—which may lead you on to a third, fourth, fifth, or sixth wonder. I hope you will never be led to '*wonder and perish*.'"[1]

Haynes maintained that his attack was on the satanic doctrine rather than Ballou, its human messenger. "Every person of discernment," protested Ballou, "must see that your design was personal."[2] To which Haynes replied, that, "If men of *discernment* could see a likeness between that and yours, I can see no ground of complaint."[3] If the doctrinal shoe fit, Ballou would be forced to wear it. Twenty-five years later Hosea Ballou can be found still contending that if the shoe does not fit, you must acquit.

How did Lemuel Haynes' Calvinism relate to slavery? Almost all the New Divinity men were anti-slavery. Again, the real question of the day was not abolition, but post-slavery society. As Calvinists, they all believed that the Trans-Atlantic Slave Trade was not merely an accident in history—they believed it was evil and not *caused* by God—but they believed that God had purposed *something* in it. They saw it as

---

[1] Ibid.
[2] Ibid.
[3] Ibid.

their duty to discern what exactly that was and then throw everything they had behind it.

To their eyes, the displacement of millions and millions of West Africans in the Trans-Atlantic Slave Trade was almost a *dispensation*. These men were postmillennial in their eschatology.[1] They longed for the millennium of a Christianized world in a Christianized age, and they saw the abolition of slavery as essential to usher in the golden era. They saw slavery in general (to say nothing of the specific crime of *manstealing,* upon which much of the slave trade was built)[2] as an old-world institution. God provided laws for it in the Old Testament, permitted and regulated it, but it was not his will. "Men were made for more noble Ends than to be Drove to market, like sheep and oxen."[3] Slavery was not God's intention for man, though it was provided for in the Old Testament, not dissimilar from polygamy. Like polygamy, they believed that the gospel was destined to overthrow this perversion of nature. In Mosaic times the people were permitted to enslave *strangers,* or outsiders, but now that the gospel age had dawned and the wall of hostility had been broken down, the church is to enslave nobody. There are no more strangers.

---

[1] #datpostmil.
[2] Haynes says: "We know that under the Levitical Oeconomy, *man-stealing* was to Be punished with Death." Newman, *Black Preacher*, 23.
[3] Ibid., 23.

For early black abolitionists, old-world slavery was most particularly exemplified in Islam. "Black Calvinism scorned Islam, which eighteenth century abolitionists, black and white, believed was the religion of West African slave-traders."[1] Muslims did not run the entire West African slave trade, but they did have a significant hand in it.[2] Human subjugation, contended black abolitionists, was part and parcel with the fabric of Islamic society, and there was no doctrinal power within Islam to overthrow it. Only Christianity could do so. Black Muslims were slave traders; black Christians were abolitionists. So much for *the white man's religion*.

Their inherent principles led the two religions in squarely opposite directions. Where Christians practiced slavery, they were inconsistent with their Christianity. "The persistence of slavery in nominally Christian times meant to black commentators that a corrupt or even false religion held sway."[3] Where Muslims did so, they were reconciled with their own system. African Muslims "traced their right to enslave people back to the Qur'an."[4] To see how deep the prophet's cave goes, primary Muslim sources tell us that Muhammad was a white man with

---

[1] Saillant, *Black Puritan*, 4.
[2] See Paul E. Lovejoy, *Transformations in Slavery: A History of Slavery in Africa, Third Edition* (New York: Cambridge University Press, 2012).
[3] Saillant, *Black Puritan*, 35.
[4] Lovejoy, *Transformations in Slavery*, 86.

black slaves—such were the abolitionist efforts of Mecca.[1] In the end, Islam offered "at best piecemeal resistance"[2]—partial, territorial, but not a *universal* resistance to slavery itself. "For literate black abolitionists Islam and Christianity were worlds apart."[3]

So far, the New Divinity men are agreed. But then comes the question of what *exactly* God was doing in the matter. This wasn't a speculative nicety for them; they felt themselves duty-bound to trace God's hand and follow his lead. Sharp disagreements ensued. Many New Divinity men believed that God's purpose in the Trans-Atlantic Slave Trade was to bring West Africans into Christian nations to hear the gospel, be converted, become equipped, and go back to West Africa to evangelize it—that is, they believed this was God's purpose for the *entire* black American population. This was of course *colonization*.

Beyond the exchange of the gospel, the mantra of many was that never the two ethnicities shall meet. Many of "the New Divinity men condemned…black and white men and women who allowed affection to cross race lines."[4] Jonathan Edwards Jr., for instance,

---

[1] See David Wood's video, "Muhammad: The White Prophet with Black Slaves," https://www.youtube.com/watch?v=tZxH4QYLRQY&t=10s.
[2] Saillant, *Black Puritan*, 28.
[3] Ibid., 27. "The experience of becoming an abolitionist was also for these Africans one of becoming an enemy of Islam." Ibid., 32.
[4] Ibid., 101.

thought that white people should rather leave their homes and lands behind than mix with black folks. He considered this to be "inconceivably more mortifying than the loss of all their real estates, I mean the mixture of their blood with that of the Negroes into one common posterity."[1] *Yuck*. Those of us with mixed children behold for ourselves the stunning beauty that comes from mixed marriages—a treasure far surpassing houses and lands.

Again, this was hardly a question of abolition; the real issue was that of post-slavery society. To these men, "black and mixed-race Americans came to represent just as much a threat to the republic as did slavery and the slave trade."[2] Thus many New Divinity men shared the beliefs of Thomas Jefferson and held that God desired to remove the entire black population from American soil. It would have been a heart-rending judgment, one which we are glad God did not execute upon this land for the sins of so many of its fathers.

Well, spoiler alert, *they were wrong*. Colonization didn't work. It was not God's will to uproot an entire population and replant them back across the Atlantic. Thus, an unwanted colony was left within America, a sort of shadow population. America, *home*

---

[1] Ibid., 100.
[2] Ibid., 101.

of the free, was left with internal colonization and second-class black citizenship.

Will Haynes shy away from Calvinism itself, concluding it to be a racist system? Nay! He will charge deeper into Calvinism than his Calvinistic opponents and show them what Calvinism is really made of. What he and men like Equiano believed God was doing was something far greater than the evangelization of West Africa. Yes, some would go back and preach the gospel, but God was demonstrating the power of the gospel on an enormous scale by birthing mixed, post-slavery churches and free societies that lived in peace and harmony. Former masters and former slaves worshipping God together and living in benevolent brotherhood is a rare fruit indeed, and one that only the cross can produce. They believed the gospel was the only force powerful enough to bring about such breathtaking results. These were intense debates, and in the fray Lemuel Haynes was making stunning advances within Calvinism.

In fact, all early black abolitionists were Calvinists. "Not until around 1815 would African American authors, such as John Jea, explicitly declare themselves against Calvinism and for free-will religion."[1] Nineteenth century abolitionists departed

---

[1] Ibid., 4.

from the well-trodden paths of their forebears. Their "use of the Bible wrote slavery and slaves out of providential history in a way that Haynes and his peers would have found alarming."[1] In other words, if one does not affirm that God sovereignly brought the black population to America, *how can one explain the ongoing black presence in America?* The best that they could come up with was that the black population was merely an unfortunate and random byproduct of this tragedy.

Haynes believed that God *intended* the Trans-Atlantic Slave Trade for the purpose of bringing about mixed free churches and societies that glorified God through the power of the gospel; his Calvinism drove his belief. The Arminianism of later abolitionists did not allow them to say this. They did not believe that there was any divine design whatsoever in the slave trade. They believed (though they may not have put it in these terms) that evil had simply gotten away with something. Their theology left them with a bankrupt abolitionism that couldn't deal with the black population in post-slavery America. Because they believed the slave trade was an anomaly in history, they were forced to believe that the subsequent black population was also "an anomaly in American society,"[2] *without divine purpose.*

---

[1] Ibid., 185.
[2] Ibid.

They had no doctrinal footing, no doctrinal teeth. In forsaking Calvinism, their house was left to them desolate.

Another consequence of free-will theology in abolitionism was this:

> Between 1810 and 1820, black authors began expressing an understanding of the slave trade and slavery informed not by Calvinist providentialism, but by free-will evangelicalism. The slave trade appeared not as an ancient sin in which African elites and traders had long been involved, but as a modern European and American depravity alien to Africa… The hand of the predestining God disappeared from the slave trade and slavery.[1]

What hand? The sovereign hand that was abolishing all forms of slavery through this crescendo of human wickedness in the Trans-Atlantic Slave Trade. Instead, they romanticized Africa as a paradise which had been corrupted by Western slavery. The urgent need West Africa had of the gospel and its sweet influences was consequently pacified.

---
[1] Ibid., 177-78.

Haynes, contrariwise to the free-will generations to come, saw intense design everywhere. "Haynes' ideals threatened not just slavery, but separation and segregation."[1] The Black Puritan was *dangerous* to ongoing racism in all its forms. When colonization was embraced, it influenced later abolitionism. Separation inevitably became a necessary, if not a *good* thing. Haynes' pointed Calvinism created problems for this kind of thinking. He was a true Calvinist, "notwithstanding the racism of most of its adherents."[2] Instead of fleeing from the tradition, he went deeper into its essence. He snatched the weapon from their hands and showed them how to use it. "He made momentous advances in New Divinity thought…He wrote a new chapter in American Calvinism."[3]

The New Divinity men, as Calvinists, were intensely focused on the glory of God (think of John Piper, who was most influenced by Jonathan Edwards). They looked for the glory of God in all things. Edwards and the men who followed him were earnest in their belief that all creation displayed the glory of God, and believed it was their duty to discern and acknowledge God's splendor in "this

---

[1] Ibid., 187.
[2] Ibid., 107.
[3] Ibid., 115-16.

glorious theater," as Calvin puts it.[1] Haynes took this truth and mined the anti-slavery, anti-racism, and pro-black treasures of Calvinism, powerfully bringing them forth.

He argued that oppression was just this very thing: *not* acknowledging the glory of God. Whether manifested in slavery or racism or colonization, or prejudiced fear of a black population, all such things are the very opposite of what Calvinism calls for. To acknowledge the glory of God is to recognize and honor *the image of God* wherever it is found, and where is that most clearly manifested but in *image bearers?* To love the oppressed and oppose the sinfulness of rejecting the image of God in other people is true Calvinism, argued Haynes. Celebrating the glory of God in butterflies, but not in *image bearers,* is but a larvae Calvinism; under Haynes, Calvinism spread its wings as the majestic Monarch it was destined to become.

The New Divinity men were highly suspicious of human pride and selfishness. Were the desire for freedom merely a longing for selfish living, they were disposed to stifle it. Haynes argued that the desire for earthly freedom was not necessarily selfish desire, but was for believers a longing to worship God fully.

---

[1] John Calvin, *The Institutes of the Christian Religion* (Peabody: Hendrickson Publishers, 2014), 1.5.8.

A free life is in fact the biblical ideal.[1] John Calvin says, "It is not very sound theology to confine a man's thoughts so much to himself, and not to set before him, as the prime motive of his existence, zeal to illustrate the glory of God."[2] Haynes argued that this was the very thing that animated the desire for freedom in Christians. The glory of God was to be sought through the dignity only a free society can offer. In this way, his puritanism dovetailed with his politics:

> Haynes carried the religious insight that freedom came from Christ into both an abolitionist understanding of black freedom and a republican understanding of the necessity of securing freedom for all members of a commonwealth. A more forceful attack on slavery articulated within the Christian and republican traditions was scarcely imaginable.[3]

He essentially asked his contemporaries, Is *your* doctrine of regeneration, O professing Calvinists, strong enough to cross these lines or is it not? He

---

[1] "That we may lead a peaceful and quiet life, godly and dignified in every way" 1 Tim. 2:2; "Live as people who are free" 1 Pet. 2:16; "If you can gain your freedom, avail yourself of the opportunity" 1 Cor. 7:21.
[2] John Calvin, *Tracts and Letters* (Edinburgh: Banner of Truth Trust, 2009), 1:33.
[3] Saillant, *Black Puritan*, 63.

called for benevolence on all sides, from both former slave owners as well as former slaves. The black Calvinist believed that sovereign grace was strong enough to bring both parties together in peace. His opponents were inconsistent. "A more forceful challenge to the slave trade, to slavery, and to racism could hardly have been articulated within the Calvinist tradition."[1]

Men like Olaudah Equiano, Lemuel Haynes, and Timothy Dwight were the most consistent Calvinists of their day. As to being Calvin's true heirs, Timothy Dwight believed that the abolition of slavery and the bringing together of free societies was a historical movement on par with the Reformation itself. Black freedom was, as Lemuel might have it, *The Reformation Further Extended*. To be black and Reformed, it seems, is not so strange after all.

#MERICA

What comes to mind when you hear that word? Confederate flags and cheap beer, I shouldn't wonder. But I bet none of my readers thought of the South—South Trinidad, that is. As it turns out, there was a group of American slaves who fled the States and fought with British forces in the War of 1812,

---
[1] Ibid., 114.

and were subsequently given land to settle in southern Trinidad. And they were called—wait for it—*Merikins*.

The Merikins fought a false America, an America that professed liberty and justice for all, *except for y'all*. And so, in defecting to Britain they were in a very real sense fighting a false America. They saw the hypocrisy of it all, contending for white American slaves while black American slaves were ignored. The Merikins saw that the land of the free was in reality the home of the slave.

Lemuel Haynes surpassed them. He not only fought the false America, based on its own principles, but he fought for the real America, based on its principles. He planted his feet, stood his ground, and turned his mighty tusks on anyone who tried to bully him. He was unintimidated. He was a true American; as an unsung hero, perhaps *the* truest American. And thus, I will call him *the Merican*.

He was handed "a legacy of racism in both Calvinist and republican thought"[1] and forged it into "a distinctly American confluence of faith and politics."[2] Forging together the young country's founding forces, he contended that "oppression [in all its forms] was wrong by both republican and

---
[1] Ibid., 20.
[2] Ibid., 86.

Calvinistic standards."[1] A most truly American answer to the problem.

The free black population in America had become an unwanted thing, not dissimilar to Haynes' own existence. Disowned from birth, he was the offspring of a sinful situation. In order to forget the act, his mother abandoned him and his father forsook him. The likeness to the American black population as a whole is striking.

He didn't ask to be here, yet here he was. Why should he suffer for it? That happens to be precisely our argument against abortion—*it's not the baby's fault*. It wasn't the fault of the black population in America, so why should they be blamed, or unwanted, or suffer for the sins of their oppressors? They had been looted, stolen, and brought against their will over shark infested waters, passing through suffering and living horror, only to become an unwanted nuisance in a strange land. And, God forbid we need to spell it out beloved, *it was not their fault*. The free black population became an unwanted child from past sin whose very existence threatened to expose the evil. Haynes' answer was to face the facts and give the gospel free reign in reconciling all.

In his genius, Lemuel Haynes saw parallel experiences between the Revolutionary patriots and

---

[1] Ibid., 117.

black slaves. Without equating their sufferings, he saw that *both* groups had tasted the bitter cup of tyranny and oppression to one degree or another. The similarities were unmistakable for Haynes; he had in his own experience taken part in both forms of oppression. His "very duality allowed him to see and experience the double-meanings of 'America.'"[1] Tracing God's hand, he believed the lesson was clear: to treasure a thorough freedom, to fight for it, and to become extremely, yea, *dangerously* learned, armed with knowledge and truth. He believed this was the very thing God was teaching early America.

Here we are, the offspring, many generations later. Is Haynes' America the America of a dream long passed out of reach? Or is it an America that may yet be future? Were it possible, may it be so. Yet I will say this: May it never be that we are needful of another lesson in tyranny and slavery. May it be that God doesn't send another scourging our way, to teach us the delicacy and preciousness of freedom, the utter importance of benevolence, and the absolute power of the gospel of Jesus Christ.

---

[1] James Melvin Washington, quoted in Newman, *Black Preacher*, xi.

THE END OF THE MATTER

In the end, his republicanism, his puritanism, and his skin cost him his pulpit. He was dismissed in 1818, when the tide had turned politically, theologically, and racially. Speaking of himself, he says, "He had lived with the people of Rutland for 30 years, and they were so sagacious that at the end of that time they found out that he was *a nigger,* and so turned him away."[1] No matter; the minister is called to suffering. He considered himself an heir of the preachers of old:

> The history of the preachers of the gospel in every age of the world, afford distressing evidence in proof of the point before us. The imprisonment of a Rutherford, a Baxter, the sufferings of a Manton, Flavel, Whitefield, and their contemporaries, evince this truth, that opposition to the servants of Christ is not an accidental thing… They will not give up the cause, come life, or come death. This rendered Luther, Melancton, Huss, Jerome, Polycarp, Wickliffe, and a thousand others

---

[1] Ibid., xiv.

invincible to all the flatteries and intrigues of wicked men and devils.[1]

His deathbed was a scene of great instruction. "He was rapidly ripening," says Cooley, "by progressive sanctification to join with holy beings in another world."[2] A friend asked, "Shall I stay by you?" The old saint replied, "Oh yes, I want your company for all eternity."[3] He longed for the fast-approaching day, and to be with all the saints. "I shall there see…Owen!"[4] Minsters clustered about him. "They sought to comfort him, or more likely, to catch the falling mantle of the departing saint."[5] A great champion in Israel was passing, and many a young preacher wished that even the fringes of his lengthening shadow might fall on them before the end.

He held time precious during life—"One hour of our present life is of more consequence to fit for future scenes than all eternity"[6]—and was granted much of it, beyond the measure of his generation. But eventually his allotted measure had run its determined course; God called him home, an old

---

[1] Ibid., 183, 93.
[2] Cooley, *Sketches*, 257.
[3] Ibid., 305.
[4] Ibid. The more I learn, the more I love this brother.
[5] Ibid., 311.
[6] Ibid., 132.

man, ripe in years and good works. After he passed into the blessed realms, his son wrote, "Our father was happy in death; his sun set clear."[1] They took up his body and buried it. But *it will rise again*, with him in it. His tombstone bears a simple inscription, but it was later found that he had, as a young man, written in his own hand the following:

An epitaph to be put upon my tombstone.

HERE LIES THE DUST OF A POOR HELL-DESERVING SINNER, WHO VENTURED INTO ETERNITY TRUSTING WHOLLY ON THE MERITS OF CHRIST FOR SALVATION. IN THE FULL BELIEF OF THE GREAT DOCTRINES HE PREACHED WHILE ON EARTH, HE INVITES HIS CHILDREN, AND ALL WHO READ THIS, TO TRUST THEIR ETERNAL INTEREST ON THE SAME FOUNDATION.

LEMUEL HAYNES
WHO DIED[2]

September 28, 1833

---

[1] Ibid., 310.
[2] Ibid., 312.

CONCLUSION

I fear that we live in a very unlearned age. We are a shallow people, and have much to learn. Who will answer the call? These old ministers held great eschatological hopes of what God was doing in America and in the world. Jonathan Edwards looked forward to the millennium as a time when there would be black and native "divines," *theologians and preachers*. Even now, thanks to unexpected influences like Reformed hip hop,[1] an army of minority preachers bearing the Reformed mantle seems to be in the making.

"The story," says Cooley, "of the Saturday evening sermon and the chimney corner education of Lemuel Haynes is worthy of being told on the banks of the Senegal in the days of the millennium."[2] Whatever our own take on the millennium may be, we say with joyful certainty that the story of the Black Puritan is worthy of being told in prestigious seminaries and under street lights in every hood—and, by God's grace, wherever the two shall meet.

---

[1] Mark Dever mentions this as one reason for the Reformed resurgence we have seen in recent years. See the following lecture. "Where Did All These Calvinists Come From?" http://www.capitolhillbaptist.org/sermon/where-did-all-these-calvinists-come-from.

[2] http://earlyamericansermons.org/Content/Files/1808haynes1sam18-9.xml.

Made in the USA
Las Vegas, NV
27 January 2021

16594772R00033